VICTORY IN LIFE'S PROBLEMS

To Help you in the Hurting

by Evangeline Carey

authorHOUSE®

AuthorHouse™
1663 Liberty Drive
Bloomington, IN 47403
www.authorhouse.com
Phone: 1-800-839-8640

First published by AuthorHouse 2/19/2010

ISBN: 978-1-5850-0104-0 (sc)

Behold I have refined you but not with silver. I have
chosen you in the furnace of affliction. (Isaiah 48:10)

Printed in the United States of America
Bloomington, Indiana

This book is printed on acid-free paper.

These poems are written to encourage anyone who is hurting mentally, physically or spiritually. They are written to help you look beyond your circumstances to a God who loves you always and beyond.

Special thanks to my wonderful husband
and three children who stood with me
in my fiery furnace.
Evangeline Carey

TABLE OF CONTENTS

FOREWORD

This book consists of poems that I have written over a period of ten years or more and Scriptures from God's Holy Word. They are for those days when you feel spiritually weak, afraid, upset, disturbed, or just out of touch with God and man. I pray that they will lift you up so that you won't be looking outward at your circumstances, but upward to a God who loves and cares for you always and beyond.

Evangeline Carey

INTRODUCTION

Then Nebuchadnezzar, the King was astonished,
and rose up in haste and spoke,
and said unto his Counselors, "Did not we cast three men
bound into the midst of the fire?"
They answered and said unto the King,
"True, O King." He answered and said,
"Lo, I see four men loose, walking in the midst of the fire,
and they have no hurt; and the form of the fourth is like
THE SON OF GOD."
Daniel 3:24-25

A SPECIAL WELL

There was a well
that ran down...
down...
down...
down...
deep down
into spiritual soil.
It was a deeper well
that tapped into
the resources of my God,
And because I drew from it,
I was blessed with
priceless treasures:
strength,
hope,
divine peace,
and eternal life!

VISION

God molds each tiny snowflake,
giving it its own
distinct character,
distinct variance,
distinct beauty.
He determines where they will
fall in the vast scheme of things.
He has command.
Yes, this is His domain
for He alone is Lord,
and does everything,
each and everything
oh so very well.
It is He who takes those
shimmering ice crystals
and blankets the sky,
and at His given time,
they fall to the earth
causing man to stand in awe.

Surely this great God Almighty
can control my life better than I!

GOD KNOWS ME!

God knows me
Through and through.
He knows me,
Everything that I do.
He knows me!
He's my God!
He knows my thoughts.
He knows my heart!

MY LIFE!

I stood on a lonely hill
Peering into the heavens,
Pensively considering my life
And the roads that lay ahead.
Yes, the choice was mine
As to what my life should be,
No other souls could share.
It was entirely up to me.
I had to choose the path that I would travel
As I carved my niche under the sun,
As I scaled the highest mountain
And plowed the lowest valleys.
Yes, the choice was mine
As to what my life should be,
For I must live with myself
Even if no one else lives with me.
My choice is to live my life
As a child of God!

THANK YOU, GOD!

Thank you, Lord
for being such a wonderful
and true friend,
for the peace and love
that you constantly send,
for the hope and joy
that mark my way,
for every moment you
walk with me
each hour of the day!

I LOVE YOU, GOD!

You accent the positive in life,
the beauty, and the good.
You crown me with love and kindness
until my cup overflows.
I study your Word and Promises
and I am refreshed,
renewed in strength,
and able to go another mile.
Mole hills do not become mountains
when I talk with YOU,
for you help me to see more clearly,
to stop and be grateful for the little things in
life.
Although you're sometimes disappointed in
me,
YOU still appreciate my humanity.
That's why when I speak of YOU,
I speak of LOVE.
When I think of YOU,
My thoughts perceive LOVE,

And when I love YOU,
I'm more than blessed!

REJOICE! REJOICE!

There is laughter in my soul
and joy in my heart,
since God rescued my life
and gave me a new start.
There is purpose in my life,
Yes, so much hope just for me,
since He liberated my broken spirit
and truly set me free.
I am no longer under my burdens
and I see that God is still on His throne.
Since I let Him hold my heart,
I never have to walk alone.

FAITH

I knew that I could trust my God
when storm draped clouds arose in my life
and shook the very tranquility of my soul.
I knew that I could trust Him,
and I did!
I knew that I could talk to my God
when the albatross of loneliness,
tore at the very fiber of my well-being.
I knew that I could talk to Him,
and I did!
I knew that I could depend on my God
in times of sorrow,
in times of uncertainty,
in times of sickness,
in times of despair.
I knew that I could depend on Him,
and I did!

IN GOD

In God,
I am complete.
In Him,
I am whole.
I can meet life's many challenges
And come forth as pure gold.
God walks
Right by my side.
He shows me the way,
And even through
the raging storms,
I see the beauty in the day!

A SPECIAL PRAYER

Dear God:
I am awed by your long suffering
and patience in dealing with me,
How you are quick to comfort,
And to reward my weakness with your
support.
Your love is forever present before me,
and I do find that nothing that I do or say,
keeps it from touching me.
You stand firm by your word, Lord
even in such a changing world,
and though everything else shifts around me,
I can count on YOU to remain the same!
Thank You, Lord!
A-men.

REASSURANCE

Even in the deep dark valleys,
the desert places of life,
there is a special peace that I feel
when I am passing through.
It reassures me all the day
that My God truly loves me too.
His gentle touch,
like the brush of angels' wings,
and quiet voice
come when I'm alone,
to reassure my broken heart
that I'm indeed His own.

GOD IS WITH ME!

I was not alone in my trials,
for God was with me.
He took me by the hand
and consoled me patiently.
I was not alone
when my friends left my side,
for God was with me
and in His arms I did hide.
I am never alone
when life's billows roll,
For God is always near
and comforts my soul.

THE STORM WILL PASS!

The storm will pass!
It cannot last,
because God is still on the throne.
He sees your tears,
He knows your fears,
And will comfort you while your mourn.

GOD CARES
FOR YOU!

Cry no more
In your despair,
Lift your heart
To a God who cares.
He knows your needs
And He's there for YOU.
He will lift your load
And see you through!

TO COMFORT YOUR HEART!

There are things you can tell God
That you can tell no other soul,
Help that you can get from Him,
When circumstances are beyond
your control.
You do not have to worry
About what you say to Him.
You can talk and talk
Until your sorrows dim.
God will keep in His bosom,
Your private inner thoughts,
And give you perspective
On the rainbows you have sought.
When you talk to God,
You are sharing with a friend,
One who is constant,
On whom you can depend!

A PRAYER FOR A FRIEND!

I pray for you, My Friend,
that God will keep your steps
day by day moving toward Him,
that He will give YOU rest
and His wonderful peace,
as you trust in His promises
to love and keep you,
as you worship and delight in Him.
I pray for YOU, My Friend,
that you will so often be able
to slow down your life,
and enjoy the beauty
to be found in God's creations.
I pray for YOU always, My Friend!
Please always pray for me!

THE GARMENT OF PRAISE

My God put on me
the garment of praise
in the midst of my despair.
He wrapped me in His loving arms
and let me know His care.
He did not leave me alone
even when friends left my side.
My God spread His mighty wings,
and in them I did hide.
He lifted my spirit to a higher plane
as I had blessed fellowship with Him.
Yes, God nurtured and loved me
when my life became dark and grim!

TAKE TIME

Take time
to be alone with God,
to reflect on His goodness,
and He'll renew your heart.
Take time
to praise His Holy Name,
to commune with your Savior,
and you'll never be the same!

YOU ARE NOT ALONE!

Friends and loved ones come
while you are dealing with pain,
but they all go away.
The nights are long,
and then it's a new day.
Still your heart is heavy,
You have to face your fears,
Your eyes may be swollen,
drowned in tears.
You are not alone,
in this your time of grief.
God's divine presence
will flood you with His peace!

YOU ARE LOVED!

You are loved
by a wonderful, merciful,
and loving God,
Who sees all
and knows your heart.
He sees those trials,
the valleys and desert places too,
All life's raging agonizing storms
that you must go through.
Oh lift up your head, My Child,
You can! You can...
For you are loved
by the Creator of man!

MY PRAYER FOR YOU!

May God give you a measure of faith
Where you stagger not at His promises,
Where there is no room for worry or doubt,
So that when troubles are pressing on every
hand,
You will know what complete faith in Him is
all about!
May God give you a measure of faith that
will keep you,
Yes, keep you constantly in His will,
So that when you go through the valleys so
low,
You will render prayer and praises still!
May God grant you a faith that can be used
to deliver you,
When your heart is dark with pain,
So that you can rest in the fact that He is
your Savior
And trust in Him again and again!

HELP FOR THE WEARY!

You must let go of your problems
And let God solve them,
Indeed you must!
If you're to find rest for your weary soul,
You must let Him take control,
Then watch as He builds your trust.
You must rest in the love
Of the mighty God above,
When your broken heart yearns for release,
You must let Him come your way
And bring hope to your day,
And grant YOU His wonderful peace!

GOD AND HIS CHILDREN

God enriches the soul of His children
through prayer.
He blesses their heart
through praise.
He teaches them about Himself,
through His precious Word.
And He supplies their needs,
through their fellow man!

NEAR TO THE HEART OF GOD!

Thank YOU
for being so very near, Dear Lord,
As I travel earth's foreign land.
Thank YOU for being my comforter,
The one who holds my hand.
I can go through the many test of life
Because you are my constant guide,
Who leads me through the dark draped
clouds
Safely to the other side.
It is indeed so wonderful
To know that I have a friend in YOU,
Who will never leave me alone,
And will always see me through!

GOD'S LOVE!

The depth of God's love
Truly transcends,
Even the imagination
Of mortal men.
And the hope He brings
Is a piercing light,
That illuminates
The darkest night.
And O the peace
That only He can give,
So gently inspires
The soul to live!

EBENEZER
(Stone Of Help)

It is during the mid-nights of the soul,
the winter seasons of our walk with God,
that He sends the sunshine of His grace
to warm our spirit,
to lift our heart up, up, up
out of the miry pit of despair to a higher
plateau,
where we can look beyond our circumstances
and see His might and power,
His love, and care for us always and beyond.
It is during these agonizing times
that His Divine Presence:
so holy and faithful,
so loving and merciful,
infiltrates our whole being and gives us new
life.
It is then that we are strongest
in our time of weakness,
and can declare to our fellow man,
"The joy of the Lord is my strength!"

OF JOY AND GLADNESS

Let us hear joy and gladness, Lord
So that we may share them
With our fellow man,
So that we may give hope,
Brighten someone's way,
And spread your love where ever
we can.

LIFE

Life is not so lonely
When we share it with a friend,
When we reach out to others
With a helping hand to lend,
When we comfort a broken heart
Or just give a tender smile,
Life is not so lonely
When with others we walk the mile.

TO SHARE

We need to share the joy
To be found in each passing day.
We need to touch someone with a smile
As we meet others along the way.
We need to love, and love, and love
And know that others love us too,
These things bring out the beauty of life
All the year through.

GOD LIFTED ME UP

God lifted my soul to a higher plane
In the midst of my despair,
Lack of hope and peace
Marked my every step and care.
I needed again the joy of my salvation,
I needed to see His love,
I needed to find that blessed assurance
That comes from God above.
But you see, God did not leave me.
It was I who neglected to pray!
I did not study His precious Word
And therefore fell by the way.
But He brought me back to Himself,
Now, I know that I can stand.
I can walk through this valley,
Because He holds my hand.

IN HIM
PUT YOUR TRUST!

Never give up!
Keep pressing on!
Strive to win the prize,
Tap hidden resources
you are shown.
Never say, "I can't!"
Always say, "I must!"
God will help you meet
the challenge,
In Him put your trust!

SOLITUDE

There are times
When we need to be alone
To look within,
To weigh our goals
And aspirations
In this world of mortal men.
We have to see
Where we are going,
As well as where we've been,
For we must be prepared
To meet life's challenges,
Or whatever it may send.

TRIALS

It is the trials of our faith
That can plant our feet solid
In God's way,
For through these trials
We can come to know
That indeed He is faithful,
And through our prayers,
We can come to know
That indeed He is God!

GOD THE SOLID ROCK!

God is a solid rock of faithfulness
right in the middle of our pain,
planted so firm and true.
He is a very present help
there to get us through.
The storm clouds may open wide
with their dousing bounty
and soak us to the heart,
but there to wipe our tears away
is a very caring God!

THE REST OF FAITH

There was a problem
that littered my life,
Crushing and debilitating,
Bringing so much trouble and strife.
It pressed and pressed me
on every side,
The battle was fierce,
Gray skies wide.
Living a life already
obedient to God,
I knew I could go to Him,
I knew it in my heart.
First, I searched the Scriptures
for similar issues,
Grabbed a promise or two,
Pleaded those edicts
As given to me and you!
Weak but determined,
In God's spirit I fell on my knees,
Praying in faith

With intense pleas.
My soul stretched out
to a Mighty God,
Who knew my pain,
The condition of my heart.
God solved this problem
Right away,
Brought peace and hope,
A sparkling new day.
He answered
As I rested in Him,
The SON filtered through,
My life no longer grim.

THE FIGHT OF FAITH

There was another situation
that demanded so much more,
I had to fight through on my knees,
In order to score.
I had to persist in my efforts,
Prevail and pray through,
Again and again
I sought what to do!
The answer did not come
the first time or third,
I had to claim His promises
Plead His Word.
I took as my guide, Luke 11:5-9
And Matthew 26:44,
I knocked and knocked
At my Savior's door.
The Holy Spirit said,
"Pray through! Pray through!
God is hearing,
There is hope for you!"

I wet my pillow with my tears day and night
Before my Lord and King,
Knowing that attainment
Only He could bring.
I wrestled in my prayers
Knowing that I would eventually win,
Because only God could bring victory,
He'd already conquered sin.
I prevailed and travailed,
Pleaded and cried,
And when I didn't know what else to say,
The Holy Spirit took my side.
The final problem solved,
I obtained my plea,
Yes, using the fight of faith,
God won the battle for me.

GOD CARES!

It is the deep winding valleys of life
Yes, the trials that prick us on every side,
That help mold our being and give us
character,
That mature us in our walk with
The Heavenly Father,
As they teach us patience through
experience,
And cause us to reach to a wonderful,
merciful God
Who loves us and truly cares.
These valleys caress the very essence of life.
They cause us to seek strength, hope, and
divine fortitude
From God who proved to be faithful in times
of trouble,
From God who walked where we must walk,
And has indeed felt our cringing pain.
It is easy to dwell on the mountain top
Where all seems right with the world,
But God suffers us to travel through the

valleys so low
Where dark clouds hover and shake the very
tranquility of our soul.
These valleys create fertile soil in our hearts
To grow the Fruit of His Spirit: goodness,
meekness, temperance, long suffering, joy,
peace, gentleness, love, and faith!

REFLECTIONS

Reflect on the good
Found in each passing day,
Thank God for His mercy
As daily you pray,
For God is faithful,
And will render to you,
All that you need
To refresh you anew.

IN THE HURTING...!

Listen to The Sovereign God in your
darkness,
Stay in the shadow of His hand.
Hush! Shhhh!
In quietness take a stand.
He wants to speak to YOU,
And you have to be quiet to hear.
Hush! Shhhh!
A Merciful God is near.
Now, just share your pain with Him alone,
While on this rocky road you trod,
Then take time to listen
As He speaks to your heart.
He has words for someone else
Who's in darkness too.
O, Sweet Messenger,
God wants to use just YOU!
He will make you light in your sister's
or brother's night,
So just listen to Him now.

Shhhh! Be quiet!
He'll make a way somehow!

I MUST NOT FORGET
MY GOD!

I must not forget my God
In the clutter of everyday living,
But I must take time
To commune with Him
Through prayer, praises,
And reading His Holy Word.
I must not forget my God
In the clutter of everyday living,
Because I need Him
Much more than He ever needed me!

WHAT KIND OF CHRISTIAN ARE YOU?

Are you a thoroughfare
through which beautiful blessings flow?
Can others see our Savior in you,
No matter where you go?
Or are you a hindrance to the redemptive
work of our Lord,
A menacing mighty clog,
Who plug up the healing fountain
of a Merciful, Loving God?

LET GOD BLESS YOU!

Let God bless you!
Release your faith in Him!
The clouds may be dark and menacing,
Pregnant with the bounty of pain,
Still, let your faith in God flourish,
Only He can hold back the rain.

RISE AND SHINE!

Rise and shine, O Christian?
The world is dark with pain,
Shine the light of God's love,
Bless in this storm of rain.
Rise and shine, O Christian!
Let others see Jesus in YOU,
People are crying all around,
They need a life brand new.
Rise and shine, O Christian!
Come now into the fray,
God wants to use YOU,
To show someone the way!

THE LOVE OF GOD!

Dear God,
I was majoring in the minors
before YOU came into my life,
I was focusing on dead-end streets
wasting my time on things
that only bring pleasure for a season
and loneliness for what seems like a lifetime.
But YOU gave me a new point of reference
and helped me to look beyond myself
and share the beauty and the good
found in truly loving and being loved.
Now, my world has balance,
It has pleasure, hope,
It has joy and happiness,
and most of all,
It has YOU, Lord!

GOD'S UNCONDITIONAL LOVE

She was immersed in her own secret
desolation,
her own private hell, as she stood peering out
into the distance with profound sadness,
brooding eyes, and trembling lips.
Unruly emotions and wayward bombastic
thoughts
flitted through, rifling even more
the sanctity of her inner peace.
Even though a dazzling sunset
with a brilliant reddish-orange hue blanket
the sky,
she could not see.

She could not appreciate the awesome
beauty
of God's hand in nature,
because she was in the throes of bone-jarring
vile pain
that filtered through her whole being,
that littered and weighed her heart.
In fact, she reeked of that pain
as tainted pesky memories marked,
and then unwrapped the still bleeding
wounds
of psychological and physical abuses
that she suffered so many years ago.
The scarring of these abuses still reaped
havoc in her life.
She had a hole in her soul,
a chasm so wide that it eroded and licked up
every scrap of her hope and joy.
Her raw memories stole her laughter and
gaiety,
drove her to long bouts of deep shattering
depression,
and flung her into a bottomless black pit of
despair.
She tangled with waning vigor forces that
demanded her all,
and left her with inexplicable emptiness,

feelings of low-self esteem,
feelings of incompleteness,
feelings of vulnerability.
She battled outrage,
blazing anger that heated like a furnace
as she contemplated the hand that life dealt
her.
She deemed it all so unfair, so unjust.
She often asked herself over and over again,
"Why? Why me? Why did it happen to
me?"
But then, one day someone special came into
her life.
He brought tenderness.

He brought compassion.
He brought understanding.
GOD picked up the shards of her heart
and patiently pieced them back together
again
with UNCONDITIONAL LOVE!

BRUISED REEDS

There are many bruised reeds
In this world today,
Lost and frustrated,
Battered along the way.
There are people,
So very many broken by life,
Shattered to the core
By troubles and strife.
So if just one person crosses
your path today,
Be gentle with your touch,
Remember that God gave you
a helping hand
And loved you so much!

THE FAMILY OF GOD

We are the family of God
Hoping to see His face by and by,
Yes, hoping to meet our Heavenly Father
One glorious day in the sky.
May I encourage you
As we travel on our way,
Or lighten the load you carry
On a very trying day?
And when I have a day of spiritual anguish,
Will you take me before our God,
And pray for all that I need
To bless and heal my heart?

SCRIPTURES

Pity me, O Lord, for I am weak.
Heal me, for my body is sick, and I am upset and disturbed.
My mind is filled with apprehension and with gloom.
Oh, restore me soon.
Psalm 6:2-3

SCRIPTURES cont.

The Lord is my light and my salvation;
whom shall I fear?
The Lord is the strength of my life,
of whom shall I be afraid?
Psalm 27:1

SCRIPTURES cont.

The Lord will give strength unto his people;
the Lord will bless his people with peace.
Psalm 29:11

SCRIPTURES cont.

But he was wounded and bruised for our sins.
He was chastised that we might have peace;
he was lashed and we were healed.
Isaiah 53:5

SCRIPTURES cont.

Then shall you call, and the Lord will answer;
you shall cry,
and He shall say, Here I am.
Isaiah 58:9

SCRIPTURES cont.

Fix your thoughts on what is true and good and right.
Think about things that are pure and lovely,
and dwell on the fine, good things in others.
Think about all you can praise God for
and be glad about.
Philippians 4:8

SCRIPTURES cont.

Don't worry about anything;
instead pray about everything;
tell God your needs and don't forget to thank him for
his answers.
If you do this you will experience God's peace,
which is far more wonderful than the human mind can
understand.
His peace will keep your thoughts and your heart quiet
and at rest as you trust in Christ Jesus.
Philippians 4:6-7

SCRIPTURES cont.

Praise the Lord! He was angry with me,
but now he comforts me.
See, God has come to save me.
I will trust in him and not be afraid.
The Lord God is my strength and my song;
he has become my salvation.
Isaiah 12:1-2

SCRIPTURES cont.

...For I have chosen you and will not throw you away.
Don't be afraid for I am with you.
Do not be dismayed,
for I am your God.
I will strengthen you. I will help you.
I will uphold you with my victorious right hand.
Isaiah 41:9-10

SCRIPTURES cont.

As for me, I look to the Lord for his help.
I wait confidently for God to save me,
and my God will certainly hear me.
Do not gloat over me, my enemies!
For though I fall, I will rise again.
Though I sit in darkness,
the Lord himself will be my light.
I will be patient as the Lord punishes me,
for I have sinned against him.
But after that,
he will take up my case and punish my enemies for
all the evil they have done to me.
The Lord will bring me out of my darkness into the light,
and I will see his righteousness.
Then my enemies will see that the Lord is on my side.
They will be ashamed that they taunted me,
saying, "Where is the Lord-that God of yours?"
With my own eyes I will see them trampled down like
mud in the streets.
Micah 7:7-10

SCRIPTURES cont.

Even though the fig trees have no blossoms,
and there are no grapes on the vine;
even though the olive crop fails,
and the fields lie empty and barren;
even though the flocks die in the fields,
and the cattle barns are empty,
yet I will rejoice in the Lord!
I will be joyful in the God of my salvation.
The Sovereign Lord is my strength!
He will make me as surefooted as a deer and bring me
safely over the mountains.
Habakkuk 3:17-19

SCRIPTURES cont.

The Lord is a shelter for the oppressed,
a refuge in times of trouble.
Those who know your name trust in you for you,
O Lord, have never abandoned anyone who searches for you.
Psalm 9:9-10

SCRIPTURES cont.

I love you, Lord; you are my strength.
The Lord is my rock, my fortress, and my savior;
my God is my rock, in whom I find protection.
He is my shield, the strength of my salvation,
and my stronghold.
I will call on the Lord, who is worthy of praise,
for he saves me from my enemies.
Psalm 18:1-3

SCRIPTURES cont.

The Lord is my shepherd;
I have everything I need.
He lets me rest in green meadows;
he leads me beside peaceful streams.
He renews my strength.
He guides me along right paths bringing honor to his name.
Even when I walk through the dark valley of death,
I will not be afraid, for you are close beside me.
Your rod and your staff protect and comfort me.
Psalm 23:1-4

SCRIPTURES cont.

That is why we have a great
High Priest who has gone to heaven,
Jesus the Son of God.
Let us cling to him and never stop trusting him.
This High Priest of ours understands our weaknesses,
for he faced all of the same temptations we do,
yet he did not sin.
So let us come boldly to the throne of our gracious God.
There we will receive his mercy and we will find grace to
help us when we need it.
Hebrews 4:14-16

SCRIPTURES cont.

But even if you suffer for doing what is right,
God will reward you for it.
So don't be afraid and don't worry.
Instead, you must worship Christ as Lord of your life.
1 Peter 3:13-15

SCRIPTURES cont.

The Lord says, "I will rescue those who love me.
I will protect those who trust in my name.
When they call on me, I will answer;
I will be with them in trouble.
I will rescue them and honor them.
I will satisfy them with a long life and give them my salvation."
Psalm 91:14-16

SCRIPTURES cont.

I look up to the mountains-does my help come from there?
My help comes from the Lord,
who made the heavens and the earth!
He will not let you stumble and fall;
the one who watches over you will not sleep.
Psalm 121:1-3

SCRIPTURES cont.

But blessed are those who trust in the Lord and have
made the Lord their hope and confidence.
They are like trees planted along a riverbank,
with roots that reach deep into the water.
Such trees are not bothered by the heat or worried by
long months of drought.
Their leaves stay green, and they go right on producing
delicious fruit.
Jeremiah 17:7-8

SCRIPTURES cont.

So now there is no condemnation for those who belong
to Christ Jesus.
For the power of the life giving Spirit has freed you through
Christ Jesus from the power of sin that leads to death.
Romans 8:1-2

SCRIPTURES cont.

Can anything ever separate us from Christ's love?
Does it mean he no longer loves us if we have trouble or
calamity,
or are persecuted, or are hungry, or cold, or in danger,
or threatened with death?
No, despite all these things,
overwhelming victory is ours through Christ,
who loved us.
Romans 8:35-37

SCRIPTURES cont.

But in my distress I cried out to the Lord;
yes, I prayed to my God for help.
He heard me from his sanctuary;
my cry reached his ears.
Psalm 18:6

SCRIPTURES cont.

The Lord hears his people when they call to him for help.
He rescues them from all their troubles.
The Lord is close to the brokenhearted;
he rescues those who are crushed in spirit.
Psalm 34:17-18

SCRIPTURES cont.

The righteous face many troubles,
but the Lord rescues them from each and every one.
Psalm 34:19

SCRIPTURES cont.

Give your burdens to the Lord,
and he will take care of you.
He will not permit the godly to slip and fall.
Psalm 55:22

SCRIPTURES cont.

If you make the Lord your refuge,
if you make the Most High your shelter,
no evil will conquer you;
no plague will come near your dwelling.
For he orders his angels to protect you wherever you go.
They will hold you with their hands to keep you from
striking your foot on a stone.
Psalm 91:9-12

Note:

The beginning Scriptures are from the King James' Version of the Bible. All others are taken from the Life Application Study Bible.

ABOUT THE AUTHOR.....

Evangeline Carey is a freelance writer with more than 400 published works at this writing. She has written and sold articles, short stories, verses, poems, and sentiments to companies across the Country. She writes Sunday School and Vacation Bible School Curriculum for Urban Ministries out of Calumet City, IL.
Evangeline is a Graduate of Indiana University with a B.A. in Sociology and Minors in Psychology and Philosophy—and Moody Bible Institute with a MA in Biblical Studies. She also worked at The University Of Chicago in Child Psychiatry Research And Development helping
them with data for proposed books and magazines. Evangeline makes her home in Northwest Indiana with her husband.